DECODING INDIA TRADE

DECODING INDIA TRADE

MANUJ ADLAKHA

Worldwide Published by
Pendown Press

PENDOWN PRESS

An ISO 9001 & ISO 14001 Certified Co.,

Regd. Office: 2525/193, 1st Floor, Onkar Nagar-A,

Tri Nagar, Delhi-110035

Ph.: 09350849407, 09312235086

E-mail: info@pendownpress.com

Branch Office: 1A/2A, 20, Hari Sadan, Ansari Road,

Daryaganj, New Delhi-110002

Ph.: 011-45794768

Website: PendownPress.com

First Edition: 2023

ISBN: 978-93-5554-537-4

Layout and Cover Designed by Pendown Graphics Team

Printed and Bound in India by Thomson Press India Ltd.

Contents

Preface

Cargopeople Logistics & Shipping Pvt. Ltd. is a leading provider of logistics solutions in India. With years of experience in the industry, we have extensive knowledge of the Indian market and culture. We are well-equipped to support international companies looking to expand their operations in India.

We understand that navigating the logistics and supply chain in the Indian market can be challenging. Thus, we would like to offer our expertise and support to help you succeed in India. We started Cargopeople Logistics to solve trust issues between the partners and to bring ease of working with international agents. There was also a significant gap in technology as logistics is an age-old industry, and we saw a need to bring new technology into this industry.

We strive to help organizations grow multifold by managing their delivery commitments and developing a robust and reliable partnership in India.

Chapter 1

Navigating the Indian Market: Understanding Indian Culture and Working with Indian Freight Forwarding Companies

Introduction

India is a rapidly growing market with tremendous potential for International businesses. The country boasts a large and rapidly growing consumer market, a highly skilled workforce and a growing manufacturing sector. However, navigating the logistics and supply chain in a foreign market can be challenging, especially for companies unfamiliar with the local culture and customs.

In this chapter, we will learn and explore the unique aspects of Indian culture and provide practical advice on how to work effectively with Indian freight forwarding companies.

Understanding Indian Culture

India is a diverse and vibrant country with a rich cultural heritage. It is a home to a diverse array of ethnic groups, languages and religions. It is essential to have a deep understanding of the cultural norms and values to build strong and lasting relationships in the market.

We are hereby listing some of the key cultural differences that companies should be aware of when doing business in India. They are:

1. **Communication:** In India, indirect communication is often preferred over direct communication. It is considered impolite to be too straightforward or confrontational. Communication is also often indirect wherein nonverbal cues, such as body language and gestures, play an essential role in conveying meaning.

2. **Relationships:** Relationships are highly valued in India. It is important to build strong relationships with business partners and customers. This can be achieved through regular interactions, personal connections and with a solid commitment towards customer service.

3. **Time:** In India, time is viewed as a flexible concept. Moreover, deadlines may not be taken as seriously

as in other countries. It is essential to be patient and flexible when working with Indian partners and to allow for additional time for tasks to be completed.

4. **Hierarchy:** Hierarchy is an important aspect of Indian culture. Decisions are often made through a top-down approach, with input from lower levels being sought only after decisions have been made at higher levels.

5. **Hospitality:** Hospitality is a deeply ingrained part of Indian culture. Visitors are greeted with warm welcome and offers of food and drink. When doing business in India, it is important to reciprocate this hospitality by showing respect and kindness to your Indian partners and customers.

6. **Respect for elders:** In India, respect for elders is a central part of cultural values. This aspect of respect can be addressed in various ways, such as giving deference to older business partners and addressing them by their formal titles.

By understanding these cultural differences, companies can more effectively navigate the Indian market and build strong and lasting relationships with their partners and customers.

Working with Indian Freight Forwarding Companies

Indian freight forwarding companies play a critical role in the logistics and supply chain in India. These companies provide valuable support and expertise to International companies looking to expand their operations in the country.

We are hereby listing some key considerations for working effectively with Indian freight forwarding companies. They are given below:

1. **Establish clear expectations:**

    An effective communication is critical when working with Indian freight forwarding companies. It is important to communicate your expectations for service, timelines and delivery in a clear manner. Moreover, it is integral to establish regular communication channels to meet your needs.

2. **Foster relationships:**

    As relationships are highly valued in India, it is important to build strong relationships with your Indian partners. Companies can strengthen their bond and relationship through regular interactions, personal connections and a strong commitment to customer service.

3. Be flexible and adaptable:

India is a rapidly changing market and so it is important to be flexible and adaptable in your approach to working with Indian partners. This may mean adjusting your processes and procedures to accommodate local customs and regulations or being open to new and innovative solutions.

4. Seek local expertise:

Indian freight forwarding companies have extensive experience and knowledge of the local market. They can provide valuable insights into the best practices and challenges of doing business in India. By leveraging this expertise, companies can more effectively navigate the local market and achieve their business objectives.

5. Be transparent:

Be transparent about pricing and services and make sure that both parties are clear on the terms and conditions of the agreement. This can help avoid misunderstandings and ensure the smooth operation of your supply chain.

6. Utilize technology:

Technology can play a critical role in the efficient and effective operation of your supply chain.

Consider working with a freight forwarder that has invested in technology, such as automated tracking and reporting systems, to enhance the customer experience and improve the speed and accuracy of information.

7. **Continuously evaluate:**

Regularly evaluate your freight forwarder's performance and ensure they are meeting your expectations. This can help identify and resolve any issues before they become significant problems.

We, at Cargopeople Logistics & Shipping Pvt. Ltd. would be happy to provide additional information and resources on this topic and answer any questions you may have.

Please let us know if you would be interested in learning more about our services and how we can support your business in India. We would also be happy to schedule a call or meeting to discuss these topics further and answer any questions you may have.

{Scan this QR code to know more about Cargopeople's Dashboard}

Choosing the Right Products and Clients for Growth in India: A Guide for International Freight Forwarders

Introduction

As International freight forwarders look to expand their operations into the rapidly growing market of India, it is critical to choose the right products and clients to support their growth. With so many options and opportunities available, it can be overwhelming to determine the best path forward. To succeed in India, freight forwarders must carefully consider their options and choose the products and clients that will support their long-term success.

Strategy 1: Focus on High-Demand Products

One of India's most important strategies for success is focussing on high-demand products. India is a rapidly growing market. There are many products in the electronics, consumer goods and textiles sector that are high in demand. By focusing on these products, freight forwarders can tap into the growing demand for these goods and position themselves for success in the market.

To determine the best products to focus on, freight forwarders should conduct market research to understand the local market and identify the products that are in high demand. They should also consider factors such as the supply chain and logistics network in place to support the transportation of these goods, as well as any local regulations and requirements that must be met.

Strategy 2: Partner with Reliable Clients

Another critical strategy for success in India is to partner with reliable clients. Freight forwarders in India are faced with a complex network of suppliers, distributors and customers. It is important to choose reliable, trustworthy and committed partners.

In order to identify the right clients, freight forwarders should consider factors such as their experience in the market, their reputation and their track record of success. They should also seek out clients that share their values and are committed to providing quality products and services to their customers.

Strategy 3: Invest in Technology and Innovation

To succeed in the rapidly evolving market of India, it is important for freight forwarders to invest in technology and innovation. This may include investing in logistics software and systems, adopting new and innovative transportation methods and exploring new business models and approaches to serve their customers.

By embracing technology and innovation, freight forwarders can streamline their operations, reduce costs and improve the overall quality of their services. This can help them to stay ahead of the competition and position themselves for long-term success in the Indian market.

Strategy 4: Focus on Quality and Efficiency

One of the most important strategies for achieving success in India is to focus on quality and efficiency. India is a country with a growing economy and expanding middle class, and consumers are becoming more discerning about the products and services they buy. In order to win their business, International logistic companies need to offer a level of quality and efficiency that is competitive with the best providers in the local market.

To achieve this, companies need to invest in technology, processes, and training that can help them deliver the highest levels of quality and efficiency. This may include investing in logistics software and systems, training employees in the latest best practices working with partners to develop innovative solutions that can help to streamline operations and reduce costs.

Strategy 5: Develop Strong Relationships with Local Partners

Another important strategy for success in India is to develop strong relationships with local partners. India is a complex and hierarchical market which can make it challenging for foreign companies to navigate the social, economic and political landscape on their own. To overcome these challenges, it is essential to work with local partners who have a deep understanding of the local market. They can also guide the company in sailing through the various obstacles that they may face.

These local partners can include freight forwarders, distributors and suppliers, as well as government agencies and other organizations. By building strong relationships with these partners, European logistic companies can gain a deeper understanding of the local market and can leverage the expertise and networks of their partners to help them succeed in India.

Strategy 6: Invest in Marketing and Branding

Another key strategy for being successful in India is investing in marketing and branding. India is a rapidly growing market with intense competition for customers. In order to stand out from the crowd, International logistic companies need to develop a strong and compelling brand that can help them to build awareness and establish themselves as leaders in the market.

It can be achieved by investing in advertising, public relations and other forms of marketing. In addition to this, the companies will be required to build a strong online presence and engage with customers through social media and other digital channels. Companies may also consider developing partnerships with local organizations and influencers. Moreover, by participating in trade shows and other events, the companies can build their reputation and connect with potential customers.

Conclusion

By following these strategies, International logistic companies can overcome the challenges of doing business in India and build a strong and successful business in this rapidly growing market. Whether through focusing on quality and efficiency, developing strong relationships with local partners, or investing in marketing and branding, companies that are prepared to invest the time and effort required to succeed in India will be well-positioned to capture the opportunities that this market has to offer.

{Scan this QR code to know more about Cargopeople's Dashboard}

Chapter 3

Growing Your Logistics Business in India - New Strategies for Success

India is a land of great opportunity for logistics companies, but it is also a market that requires unique skills and strategies to succeed. If you are an International logistics company looking to grow your business in India, there are several new strategies that you can employ to increase your chances of success.

Strategy 1: Invest in Local Talent

The first strategy to consider is investing in local talent. India has a large pool of highly skilled and motivated professionals who can bring valuable insights and expertise to your business. By hiring and training local staff, you can build a strong foundation for your operations in India and create a deeper connection to the local market.

Strategy 2: Leverage Technology

Technology is increasingly important in the logistics industry which is true in the case of India. By leveraging technology, you can increase the efficiency and reliability of your operations, reduce costs and improve the overall customer experience. Some of the most promising areas for investment include logistics management software, automation systems and data analytics.

Strategy 3: Focus on Customer Experience

Another key strategy for being successful in India is to focus on the customer experience. Indian customers are discerning and demanding and expect a high level of service and support. To meet these expectations, you need to deeply understand the local market and the needs of your customers. You should also invest in training and support programs to ensure that your employees are equipped to provide excellent service.

Strategy 4: Build Strong Partnerships

Finally, it is important to build strong partnerships with other businesses in the Indian market. It includes working with local suppliers, distributors, and other logistics providers. Building these relationships allows you to leverage their expertise and resources to improve your operations and increase your market presence. Consider forming strategic alliances with other logistics companies to expand your reach and access to new markets.

Strategy 5: Understanding the Culture

The first and most important strategy for growing your business in India is understanding the culture and diversity. India has a rich and diverse cultural heritage. It is important to respect and appreciate the values and traditions of the people you are working with.

To understand the culture, you need to learn about the customs, the etiquette and the communication styles of the people in India. You also need to understand the social and business hierarchies, and how to deal with different levels of authority and power.

By understanding the culture, you will be able to build strong and lasting relationships with your Indian partners and customers and you will be able to navigate the business landscape with ease and confidence.

Strategy 6: Building Strong Relationships

Another strategy for growing your business in India is to build strong relationships. Relationships are key to success in the Indian market, and you need to invest time and effort into building strong and lasting connections with your partners and customers.

To build strong relationships, you need to be transparent and honest in your communication, and you need to show hospitality and respect. You also need to be patient and persistent in your efforts, and you need to understand the needs and goals of your partners and customers.

By building strong relationships, you will be able to develop trust and credibility in the market, and you will be able to overcome the challenges and obstacles that you encounter along the way.

Strategy 7: Finding the Right Partners

Next strategy for growing your business in India is to find the right partners. Partnering with the right companies and individuals is key to success in the Indian market.

To find the right partners, you need to:

- Be selective and strategic in your approach

- Do your research with due diligence

- You need to assess the experience, the expertise, and the values of the companies and individuals you are working with

- Understand the strengths and weaknesses of your partners

- You need to align your goals and objectives with theirs

By finding the right partners, you will be able to leverage their expertise and experience. You will be able to build a strong and supportive network that will help you grow your business in India.

Putting It All Together

Growing your logistics business in India requires a combination of vision, determination and strategic thinking. By investing in local talent, leveraging technology, focusing on customer experience, and building strong partnerships, you can increase your chances of success and build a thriving business in this dynamic and exciting market.

So, take the leap and seize the opportunity. India is waiting for you. With the right strategies and the right approach, you can make a real impact in this vibrant and growing market, and achieve the success that you and your business deserve.

Chapter 4

Understanding the Preference for Low Cost Freight Services among Indian Freight Forwarders

Introduction

For many International logistics companies, working with Indian freight forwarders can present unique challenges, particularly concerning the preference for low-cost freight services. While cost is always a consideration for logistics companies, in India, it can often be a determining factor in the selection of a freight forwarder. In this chapter, we will explore the reasons behind this preference for low-cost freight services in India and how international logistics companies can effectively navigate this market.

The Cost-Sensitive Nature of the Indian Market

One of the primary reasons that Indian freight forwarders prefer low-cost freight services is the cost-sensitive nature of the Indian market. In many parts of India, the average income is lower than in developed countries, and businesses are looking for ways to reduce costs wherever possible. It is particularly true for small and medium-sized enterprises (SMEs), which comprise a large portion of the Indian market. These businesses often operate on tight margins and look for ways to reduce costs in order to remain competitive.

In addition to the cost-sensitive nature of the market, there are also other factors that contribute to the preference for low-cost freight services in India. For example, there are many competing freight forwarders in the market, which drives prices down as each company tries to win business. This intense competition can result in lower prices for customers, but also puts pressure on freight forwarders to offer low-cost services to remain competitive.

Navigating the Preference for Low-Cost Services

For international logistics companies, navigating the preference for low-cost services among Indian freight forwarders can present a challenge. While cost is always a consideration, it is important to remember that the lowest cost option may not always be the best option in terms of quality or reliability.

In order to navigate this market, international logistics companies should focus on delivering high-quality services at competitive prices. This can be achieved by investing in technology and innovation, streamlining operations and working closely with customers to understand their needs and requirements.

In addition, it is also important to build strong relationships with Indian freight forwarders and to understand their particular needs and requirements. This can involve regular communication and collaboration, as well as a willingness to tailor services and offerings to meet the specific needs of the Indian market.

Finally, international logistics companies should be flexible and adaptable and be prepared to adjust their strategies and approaches as the market evolves. By being proactive and responsive to the needs of the Indian market, international logistics companies can successfully navigate the challenges posed by the preference for low-cost services, and position themselves for success in this rapidly growing market.

Conclusion

The preference for low-cost services among Indian freight forwarders presents a challenge for international logistics companies. Still it is also an opportunity to differentiate themselves and build strong relationships in this market. By focusing on high-quality services, building strong relationships with customers, and being flexible and adaptable, European logistics companies can successfully navigate the Indian market and position themselves for success in this rapidly growing region.

Chapter 5

How to choose a reliable freight forwarder in India

Choosing a reliable freight forwarder in India is crucial for ensuring the smooth and efficient delivery of your products. With the rise of globalization, international trade has become increasingly important wherein freight forwarders play a crucial role in facilitating this trade. In this chapter, we will outline some important factors to consider when choosing a reliable freight forwarder in India.

1. **Experience and Expertise:**

   The first and foremost factor to consider when choosing a freight forwarder is their experience and expertise in the industry. It is essential to choose a forwarder who has a good track record of delivering goods safely and efficiently. They should also have a thorough understanding of international trade laws and regulations, as well as the customs and import/export procedures of various countries.

2. Network and Connections:

The freight forwarder you choose should have a well-established network of agents and partners in various countries. This will ensure that your goods are delivered to the destination on time and without any hassles. Furthermore, a good forwarder should have strong relationships with shipping lines, airlines and other service providers which will enable them to offer you the most competitive rates.

3. Communication:

Communication is key when it comes to freight forwarding. You should choose a forwarder who is easily accessible and responsive to your inquiries. They should also have a dedicated team of experts who can provide you with regular updates on the status of your shipment and answer any questions you may have.

4. Cost:

The cost of freight forwarding services is an essential factor to consider. Moreover, it is equally important to choose a forwarder who offers competitive rates. However, one should also keep in mind that the cheapest option may not always be the best one. It is better to choose a forwarder who offers high-quality services at a fair price rather than compromising on the quality of services to save a few bucks.

5. **Reputation:**

The reputation of the freight forwarder is another crucial factor to consider. You can check the company's online reviews, ask for references from other businesses and do some research to determine their credibility in the industry. A forwarder with a good reputation is more likely to provide high-quality services and meet your expectations.

6. **Technology:**

The use of technology has revolutionized the freight forwarding industry. It is essential to choose a forwarder who keeps up with the latest advancements. A forwarder who uses advanced tracking systems, automated invoicing and other technological tools will be able to provide you with a more efficient and streamlined experience.

7. **Flexibility:**

The nature of international trade is constantly changing. Hence, it is essential to choose a forwarder who can adapt to these changes. They should be able to offer you a range of services, such as air, sea, and road transportation, as well as warehousing and distribution services. They should also be able to provide customized solutions based on your specific needs and requirements.

Conclusion

Choosing a reliable freight forwarder in India is a critical decision for any business involved in international trade. By considering the factors discussed above, you can ensure that you select a forwarder who can provide you with high-quality services, meet your expectations and help your business succeed. A good forwarder can make a significant difference in the success of your business. So, it is best to take adequate time, undertake in-depth research and make an informed decision.

So, leap and seize the opportunity. The world is your stage. With the right strategies and the right logistics partner you can multiply your impact & income manifold to achieve the success that you and your business deserve.

Reach out to restructure your logistics strategy and take your business to the next level.

Chapter 6

National Logistics Policy of India and Considerations for International Agents

Introduction

India, with its vast geographical expanse and diverse economic activities, recognizes the critical importance of a robust and efficient logistics ecosystem for sustained economic growth and development. To address the challenges and tap into the potential of the logistics sector, the Government of India has formulated a comprehensive National Logistics Policy. This chapter aims to provide an overview of the policy and outline key considerations for international agents engaging in logistics operations in India.

The National Logistics Policy of India

1. **Enhancing logistics efficiency:** The policy aims to reduce logistics costs and improve overall efficiency through the integration of various stakeholders, modernization of infrastructure, and the adoption of advanced technologies.

2. **Promoting multi-modal transportation:** The policy encourages the development of an integrated multi-modal transportation network, leveraging road, rail, air, and waterways to provide seamless connectivity across the country.

3. **Facilitating trade and exports:** The policy aims to simplify regulatory procedures, enhance the ease of doing business, and promote trade facilitation to boost India's exports and global competitiveness.

4. **Promoting sustainable logistics:** The policy emphasizes the adoption of environmentally sustainable practices, including the use of green technologies, promoting energy efficiency, and reducing carbon emissions in the logistics sector.

Key Initiatives and Measures

To achieve the objectives outlined in the National Logistics Policy, the Government of India has introduced several key initiatives and measures, including:

1. **Development of logistics infrastructure:** The policy emphasizes the creation of world-class logistics infrastructure, including the development of logistics parks, freight corridors, and multi-modal logistics hubs across the country.

2. **Adoption of technology:** The policy encourages the widespread adoption of digital technologies such as blockchain, the Internet of Things (IoT), and artificial intelligence (AI) to streamline operations, enhance transparency, and facilitate real-time tracking and monitoring of consignments.

3. **Skill development and capacity building:** Recognizing the importance of skilled human resources, the policy focuses on skill development programs to enhance the capabilities of the workforce engaged in the logistics sector.

4. **Regulatory reforms:** The policy aims to simplify regulatory processes and reduce red tape by introducing single-window clearance mechanisms, harmonizing standards, and promoting paperless transactions.

Considerations for International Agents

Regulatory Compliance

International agents operating in the logistics sector in India need to familiarize themselves with the regulatory framework governing the industry. This includes understanding customs procedures, documentation requirements, and compliance with applicable laws and regulations, such as the Goods and Services Tax (GST) and the Foreign Trade Policy (FTP).

Infrastructure and Connectivity

While India has been actively investing in developing its logistics infrastructure, international agents must consider the existing infrastructure and connectivity when planning their operations. Understanding the availability and condition of roads, ports, airports, and railways is crucial for the efficient movement of goods across the country.

Technology Adoption

International agents should be prepared to embrace technology-driven solutions for efficient logistics operations in India. This may involve leveraging digital platforms for cargo tracking, adopting electronic documentation systems, and collaborating with local partners who are familiar with the technological ecosystem.

Cultural and Language Factors

India's cultural diversity and regional variations necessitate an understanding of local customs, languages, and business practices. International agents should consider developing strong relationships with local partners or hiring local staff who can help navigate cultural nuances and language barriers.

Sustainability and Environment

As sustainability gains prominence globally, international agents must align their operations with India's focus on sustainable logistics. This includes adopting eco-friendly practices, promoting energy-efficient transportation modes, and adhering to environmental regulations.

Chapter 7

What you need to know about Indian Customs and Tariffs

When operating in the logistics sector in India, international agents need to have a good understanding of Indian customs and tariffs.

Here are some key points to consider

1. **Customs Procedures:** International agents should be familiar with the customs procedures and documentation requirements for the import and export of goods in India. This includes understanding the necessary forms, permits, and licenses, as well as the process for customs clearance and inspections.

2. **Harmonized System (HS) Codes:** HS codes are used to classify goods for customs purposes. International agents should ensure the accurate classification of goods using the HS codes to determine applicable customs duties and taxes.

3. **Customs Duties and Taxes:** India has a complex tariff structure with various customs duties and taxes. International agents should be aware of the different types of duties, including basic customs duty, countervailing duty, and special additional duty. They should also consider any exemptions or preferential rates available under free trade agreements or special schemes.

4. **Valuation of Goods:** The valuation of goods plays a crucial role in determining customs duties and taxes. International agents should understand the methods of valuation prescribed by Indian customs authorities to ensure accurate declaration of the value of goods.

5. **Goods and Services Tax (GST):** India has implemented a Goods and Services Tax (GST) regime, which replaces multiple indirect taxes. International agents should be aware of the GST rates applicable to different goods and services and understand the compliance requirements for GST registration, invoicing, and filing of returns.

6. **Customs Duty Exemptions and Incentives:** India offers various customs duty exemptions and incentives to promote specific industries, exports, and investments. International agents should

explore these schemes, such as Duty-Free Import Authorization (DFIA), Export Promotion Capital Goods (EPCG) scheme, and Special Economic Zones (SEZs), to take advantage of cost-saving opportunities.

7. **Trade Facilitation Measures:** The Indian government has implemented several trade facilitation measures to simplify customs procedures and promote ease of doing business. International agents should stay updated on these measures, such as the Single Window Interface for Facilitating Trade (SWIFT) system, to streamline their logistics operations.

8. **Customs Brokerage:** Engaging a licensed customs broker or a logistics service provider with customs clearance expertise can significantly ease customs-related complexities. International agents should consider partnering with experienced customs brokers to ensure compliance and smooth clearance of goods.

9. **Customs Compliance and Penalties:** Non-compliance with customs regulations can lead to delays, penalties, or even the seizure of goods. International agents should ensure strict adherence to customs requirements and maintain accurate records and documentation to avoid any legal issues.

10. **Keep Abreast of Changes:** Customs and tariff regulations in India are subject to periodic updates and changes. International agents should stay updated with the latest customs notifications, circulars, and trade policies issued by the Indian customs authorities to ensure compliance and mitigate any potential risks.

By understanding Indian customs and tariffs and adhering to the applicable regulations, international agents can effectively navigate the logistics sector in India and ensure the smooth movement of goods across borders.

Chapter 8

What is GST?

From an international freight forwarder's point of view, the Goods and Services Tax (GST) in India is a significant consideration.

Here's what an international freight forwarder should pay attention to regarding GST:

1. **GST Registration:** Freight forwarders operating in India are required to register for GST if their annual turnover exceeds the threshold specified by the government. It is essential to determine the applicability of GST registration based on the nature and scale of operations.

2. **GST Rates:** Freight forwarders should be aware of the different GST rates applicable to various services in the logistics sector. The rates can vary depending on the specific services provided, such as transportation, customs clearance, warehousing, and value-added services. Understanding the applicable rates helps in accurate invoicing and compliance.

3. **Place of Supply:** GST is determined based on the place of supply, which is crucial for international freight forwarders. The place of supply can vary depending on whether the service is provided for an import, export, or domestic shipment. It is important to correctly identify the place of supply to determine the applicable GST rate.

4. **Input Tax Credit (ITC):** Freight forwarders can claim Input Tax Credit on the GST paid on inputs (goods and services) used in their business. It is important to maintain proper documentation, including tax invoices and credit notes, to support the claim for ITC. Compliance with GST regulations and documentation requirements is essential to avail of the benefits of ITC.

5. **Customs Brokerage:** Freight forwarders often act as customs brokers, facilitating customs clearance for import and export shipments. The GST implications for customs brokerage services should be understood, as they may attract GST at the applicable rates. It is crucial to accurately determine the GST liability for customs brokerage activities.

6. **Compliance and Filing Returns:** Freight forwarders must comply with the GST regulations, including timely filing of GST returns. This involves

maintaining proper records, reconciling invoices, and accurately calculating and remitting GST liability. Compliance with the GST filing requirements is essential to avoid penalties or legal consequences.

7. **Reverse Charge Mechanism (RCM):** Under the reverse charge mechanism, the liability to pay GST is shifted from the service provider to the recipient of services. Freight forwarders should understand the scenarios where RCM is applicable, such as when services are availed from an unregistered supplier, and ensure compliance with the associated obligations.

8. **E-Way Bill:** The generation of an e-way bill is mandatory for the movement of goods above a specified value under GST. Freight forwarders should be familiar with the e-way bill requirements and ensure compliance with the documentation and procedural aspects to avoid delays and penalties during transit.

9. **Audit and Assessments:** Freight forwarders should be prepared for GST audits and assessments conducted by the tax authorities. It is important to maintain accurate records, reconcile financial statements, and ensure compliance with GST

regulations to minimize any potential liabilities or disputes.

10. **Stay Updated:** GST laws and regulations are subject to amendments and updates. Freight forwarders should stay abreast of any changes through regular monitoring of government notifications, circulars, and updates from professional associations to ensure compliance with the latest requirements.

By understanding the implications of GST and ensuring compliance, international freight forwarders can effectively navigate the Indian market and provide seamless logistics services while meeting their tax obligations.

Chapter 9

Duty-Free Import Authorization

From an international agent's point of view in the logistics industry, DFIA stands for Duty-Free Import Authorization. DFIA is a scheme introduced by the Government of India to promote exports and provide duty benefits to exporters.

Here's what an international agent should know about DFIA:

1. **Eligibility:** To avail of the benefits under the DFIA scheme, an international agent should be an exporter of goods. The scheme is applicable to both manufacturer exporters and merchant exporters.

2. **Duty-Free Import:** Under DFIA, an international agent can import inputs or goods without paying customs duty. This allows them to procure goods required for the production of export products or for use in the packaging or manufacturing process without incurring additional costs.

3. **Export Obligation:** The DFIA scheme is subject to an export obligation. An international agent is required to fulfill the export obligation by exporting the manufactured goods or the goods incorporating the imported inputs within the prescribed time frame. The export obligation is typically a multiple of the duty saved on the imported inputs.

4. **Calculation of Entitlement:** The entitlement under the DFIA scheme is calculated based on the Standard Input Output Norms (SION) issued by the Directorate General of Foreign Trade (DGFT). These norms determine the quantity of inputs required for the production of a unit of export output. The duty-free entitlement is derived by multiplying the export value of the product by the duty drawback rate specified in the SION.

5. **Application and Authorization:** An international agent needs to apply to the DGFT for the issuance of a DFIA authorization. The application should include details of the intended exports, inputs required, and the associated SION. Upon approval, the DGFT issues the DFIA authorization, specifying the entitlement and other conditions.

6. **Export Documentation:** International agents must maintain proper documentation to substantiate

their exports and comply with the export obligation under the DFIA scheme. This includes maintaining records of export invoices, shipping bills, and other relevant export-related documents.

7. **Compliance and Monitoring:** International agents are required to comply with the terms and conditions of the DFIA authorization and fulfill the export obligation within the prescribed period. They should monitor their export performance and ensure the timely submission of required documents to the DGFT or the customs authorities as applicable.

8. **Transferability and Redemption:** DFIA authorizations are transferable, which means international agents can transfer them to other eligible entities. Alternatively, they can also choose to redeem the DFIA authorization by paying the customs duty saved on the imported inputs.

9. **Export Promotion Capital Goods (EPCG) Option:** International agents may also have the option to convert their DFIA authorization into an EPCG authorization. Under the EPCG scheme, they can import capital goods at a concessional customs duty rate to enhance their export production capabilities.

10. **Seek Professional Guidance:** The DFIA scheme involves various complexities and compliance requirements. International agents should seek professional advice from customs consultants, export promotion agencies, or industry associations to ensure proper utilization of the DFIA benefits and adherence to the scheme's regulations.

Understanding the DFIA scheme and its implications can help international agents optimize their logistics operations and take advantage of the duty benefits provided by the Indian government to promote exports.

Chapter 10

What is EPCG ?

From an international freight forwarder's point of view, the EPCG (Export Promotion Capital Goods) scheme in India is an important aspect to consider.

Here's an overview of the EPCG scheme and its significance:

1. **Definition and Purpose:** The EPCG scheme is an export promotion scheme introduced by the Government of India. It allows exporters to import capital goods at a concessional customs duty rate, subject to fulfilling an export obligation, with the aim of enhancing export competitiveness and upgrading production capabilities.

2. **Concessional Customs Duty:** Under the EPCG scheme, international freight forwarders can import capital goods, including machinery, equipment, tools, and components, at a reduced customs duty rate. The applicable customs duty is typically lower than the normal customs duty rates for such goods.

3. **Export Obligation:** To avail of the benefits under the EPCG scheme, international freight forwarders are required to fulfill an export obligation. The export obligation is a commitment to export a certain value of goods within a specified period, typically determined as a multiple of the duty saved on the imported capital goods.

4. **Capital Goods Usage:** The imported capital goods under the EPCG scheme must be used for the production, manufacturing, or packaging of goods for export purposes. They should be directly linked to the export-oriented production process of the international freight forwarder.

5. **Application and Authorization:** International freight forwarders need to apply to the Directorate General of Foreign Trade (DGFT) to obtain an EPCG authorization. The application should include details of the capital goods to be imported, the proposed use, and the export obligation to be fulfilled.

6. **Compliance and Monitoring:** Once an EPCG authorization is obtained, international freight forwarders must comply with the terms and conditions mentioned in the authorization. They are required to maintain proper records, submit

periodic reports to the DGFT, and fulfill the prescribed export obligations within the specified timeframe.

7. **Redemption of Export Obligation:** International freight forwarders can meet their export obligations by exporting goods directly or indirectly. They have the option to export goods manufactured using the imported capital goods, export goods on a deemed export basis, or export through a third-party export house. Proper documentation and evidence of exports need to be maintained for compliance purposes.

8. **Transferability of Authorization:** EPCG authorizations are transferable, allowing international freight forwarders to transfer them to other eligible entities. However, certain conditions and compliance requirements need to be fulfilled for such transfers.

9. **Replenishment Authorization:** In certain cases, international freight forwarders may require additional inputs for the production process. They can apply for a Replenishment Authorization (RA) under the EPCG scheme to import such additional inputs without payment of customs duty.

10. **Professional Guidance:** Given the complexity of the EPCG scheme and its compliance requirements, international freight forwarders are advised to seek professional guidance from customs consultants or trade promotion agencies. This ensures adherence to the regulations, optimization of benefits, and proper utilization of the scheme.

Understanding the EPCG scheme enables international freight forwarders to leverage the concessional customs duty benefits for importing capital goods, enhancing their export capabilities and remaining competitive in the Indian market.

Chapter 11

What is SEZ?

From an international freight forwarder's point of view, an SEZ (Special Economic Zone) is a designated geographical area within a country that offers various incentives and benefits to promote foreign direct investment, boost exports, and facilitate economic growth.

Here's an overview of SEZs from an international freight forwarder's perspective:

1. **Definition and Purpose:** SEZs are specially delineated zones within a country where specific economic regulations and policies differ from the rest of the country. The primary purpose of SEZs is to create a business-friendly environment that attracts domestic and foreign investments, encourages export-oriented industries, and fosters economic development.

2. **Infrastructure and Facilities:** SEZs typically offer well-developed infrastructure, including modern logistics parks, transportation facilities, warehousing

spaces, and customs clearance centers. These facilities are designed to streamline trade and logistics operations, providing international freight forwarders with efficient and cost-effective solutions.

3. **Customs and Duties:** SEZs often have simplified customs procedures and relaxed duty regulations compared to the rest of the country. International freight forwarders operating within SEZs can benefit from reduced or exempted customs duties, taxes, and other levies on imports and exports, thereby enhancing cost competitiveness.

4. **Export-Oriented Industries:** SEZs are primarily focused on promoting export-oriented industries. They provide a conducive environment for manufacturing, processing, and assembling goods for exports. International freight forwarders can collaborate with businesses within SEZs to handle the logistics and transportation of export goods, leveraging proximity and favorable regulations.

5. **Logistics and Supply Chain Services:** SEZs house a wide range of logistics service providers, including freight forwarders, customs brokers, transporters, and warehousing companies. This concentration of logistics expertise and services facilitates seamless

supply chain management, reducing transit times, and ensuring efficient movement of goods.

6. **Regulatory Support:** SEZs often have dedicated regulatory authorities or development agencies responsible for managing and overseeing the operations within the zone. These authorities offer support services, guidance, and assistance to international freight forwarders and businesses within the SEZs, helping them navigate regulatory requirements and resolve any operational challenges.

7. **Trade Facilitation:** SEZs emphasize trade facilitation measures to simplify processes and expedite the movement of goods. This includes implementing streamlined customs clearance procedures, providing single-window interfaces, and promoting digital platforms for trade documentation. International freight forwarders can benefit from these initiatives, resulting in smoother logistics operations and reduced administrative burden.

8. **Incentives and Benefits:** SEZs offer various incentives and benefits to attract investments and promote export-oriented activities. These can include tax exemptions, duty-free import of capital goods and raw materials, relaxed labor regulations, repatriation of profits, and access to preferential

trade agreements. International freight forwarders can leverage these incentives to offer competitive pricing and comprehensive logistics solutions to businesses operating within the SEZs.

9. **Networking and Collaboration:** SEZs often foster a vibrant business community with a concentration of diverse industries and stakeholders. International freight forwarders operating within SEZs have opportunities for networking, collaboration, and partnerships with businesses across different sectors. This can lead to increased business prospects and mutually beneficial relationships.

10. **Compliance and Reporting:** While SEZs offer various incentives, international freight forwarders must ensure compliance with the specific rules and regulations governing operations within the SEZs. This includes adhering to customs procedures, maintaining accurate records, and fulfilling reporting obligations as mandated by the SEZ authorities.

Understanding the SEZ framework and its advantages enables international freight forwarders to capitalize on the benefits and provide tailored logistics solutions within these specialized economic zones, facilitating efficient trade and maximizing business opportunities.

Chapter 12

India's Growth Story in the Logistics Sector

Introduction

India's logistics sector has experienced significant growth over the past decade, playing a vital role in the country's economic development. With its vast geographical expanse, diverse population, and expanding consumer market, India has been focusing on enhancing its logistics infrastructure to facilitate the seamless movement of goods and services. This chapter explores India's remarkable growth story in the logistics sector, highlighting key factors driving its development, the challenges faced, and the initiatives taken to overcome them.

The Need for Logistics Transformation

1. India's rapid economic growth and urbanization have led to a surge in domestic and international trade, demanding efficient logistics operations. However, the sector faced several challenges, such

as fragmented infrastructure, inadequate technology adoption, a complex regulatory environment, and inefficient supply chain networks. Recognizing the need for logistics transformation, the Indian government and industry stakeholders initiated various measures to improve the sector's performance.

Infrastructure Development

2. One of the critical components of India's logistics growth story is the development of robust infrastructure. The government has made significant investments in building new roads, expanding port capacities, modernizing airports, and constructing dedicated freight corridors. Projects like Bharatmala, Sagarmala, and UDAN have been launched to enhance connectivity and reduce transportation bottlenecks, enabling smoother movement of goods across the country.

Technology Adoption

3. To improve operational efficiency and transparency, technology has played a pivotal role in India's logistics sector. The adoption of digital platforms, cloud-based systems, Internet of Things (IoT) devices, and data analytics has enabled real-time tracking, inventory management, route optimization, and seamless information flow. Additionally, the

implementation of the Goods and Services Tax (GST) has simplified tax procedures, reducing logistical complexities and improving overall efficiency.

Warehousing and Distribution Centers

4. The growth of e-commerce and organized retail has led to an increased demand for warehousing and distribution centers in India. To meet this demand, the logistics sector has witnessed the emergence of modern and technologically advanced warehouses with features like automation, robotics, and inventory management systems. Special Economic Zones (SEZs) and logistics parks have been developed to create integrated hubs for storage, packaging, and value-added services.

Last-Mile Connectivity

5. India's logistics sector has made significant strides in improving last-mile connectivity, especially in urban areas. The rise of delivery aggregators, e-commerce logistics platforms, and hyperlocal delivery services has transformed the landscape of last-mile logistics. The adoption of electric vehicles and drones for last-mile delivery has not only improved efficiency but also contributed to environmental sustainability.

Skill Development and Training

6. Recognizing the need for skilled professionals in the logistics sector, India has taken several initiatives to promote skill development and training programs. Public-private partnerships and vocational training institutes have been established to impart industry-relevant knowledge and enhance the employability of the workforce. These efforts have resulted in a skilled talent pool capable of handling complex logistics operations.

International Trade and Connectivity

7. India's logistics growth story also encompasses its efforts to strengthen international trade and connectivity. Initiatives like the Make in India campaign, Digital India, and the implementation of single-window clearance systems have aimed to attract foreign investment, promote export-oriented industries, and streamline cross-border trade. Furthermore, India has actively engaged in regional connectivity projects like the International North-South Transport Corridor (INSTC) and the Chabahar Port in Iran, which provide alternative trade routes and access to Central Asia and Europe.

Conclusion

India's logistics sector has witnessed remarkable growth in recent years, propelled by infrastructure development, technology adoption, and policy reforms. The government's focus on improving connectivity, simplifying regulatory frameworks, and promoting digitalization has created a conducive environment for the logistics industry to thrive. However, challenges like inadequate last-mile connectivity in rural areas, high logistics costs, and limited multimodal transportation infrastructure still need to be addressed. With continued investment, innovation, and collaboration between public and private stakeholders, India's logistics sector is poised for further growth, driving the country's economic development and enabling the seamless movement of goods in the years to come.

Scan this QR code to know more about Cargopeople's Dashboard.

Schedule a discovery call.

 +919811592400

 Set up a Zoom call with us at mis@cargopeople.com